The Tao of Meow

OTHER BOOKS BY CARL JAPIKSE:

The Hour Glass

The Light Within Us

Exploring the Tarot

with Robert R. Leichtman, M.D.:

Active Meditation

Forces of the Zodiac

The Art of Living

The Life of Spirit

Healing Lines

Ruling Lines

The Tao
of Meow

by Waldo Japussy

Translated From the Original Text
by One of the Nameless Ones

ENTHEA PRESS
Columbus, Ohio

THE TAO OF MEOW
Copyright © 1990 by Carl Japikse

ISBN 0-89804-800-1

To All The Japussies,

Japixies,

& Japikses

Introduction

It is always somewhat humbling to discover that your cat, no matter how fond of him you may be, is a deeper thinker than you are.

We always knew Waldo was a superior cat, from the very first day he appeared in our lives and firmly introduced himself as "Waldo." We made the usual jokes: "Would you like us to call you Ralph?" and "So, where's your pond?" but he just smiled and endured our little pleasantries. It was only later that we learned that the name "Waldo" actually means "ruler," and that our new feline friend was merely making a statement of truth.

Over the years, Waldo has taught us a great deal about living. He is, after all, the developer of The Waldo Principle, one of the great guidelines to personal growth. Throughout his long tenure with us, Waldo has only demonstrated two faults. One was an unfortunate proclivity to break wind in our presence, which blissfully cleared up as his diet improved. The second was a neurotic habit of chewing away the fur along his hind legs—and sometimes other parts of his body as well. He would begin to clean himself, like any cat would do, and then become so intently involved in licking one spot clean that he would actually tear away the fur, leaving a raw spot in an otherwise immaculate coat. This habit of self-mortification was so strong we decided he must have been a Catholic monk in an earlier life.

Wanting to help Waldo overcome this affliction, we naturally did everything we could think of to make it worse. We took him to the vet, who attached a long, Latin name to the condition; he also gave us an ointment to rub into the raw spots Waldo had made. The ointment had a foul taste; the idea was that when Waldo began licking his favorite raw spots, he would be repelled by the foul taste of the ointment and quit mortifying himself. Which was an excellent theory, except for one consideration. It didn't work. Waldo did, as predicted, ignore the anointed spots—but at the price of starting completely new ones elsewhere on his body. What's worse—he would run and hide from us every time we called him, fearing another application of the dreaded ointment. He spent most of his time cowering under the chaise.

This effort was followed by several other, equally moronic attempts to help Waldo conquer his neuroses. Nothing worked, until the day we realized that we were so obsessed with curing our cat that we were, in fact, estranging ourselves from him. So we adopted a new strategy. We threw out the ointment, the sedatives, and the other pharmacologies and let Waldo be himself. We sat down and told him that he was a fine cat in every regard, and if he wanted to chew himself, we could learn to accept that. Instead of trying to cure him anymore, we would limit ourselves to loving him and being friends with him. And we made a special effort to make up for all the time we had lost in getting to know him.

Within a week, Waldo had stopped chewing himself. Naturally, we were delighted. But we also realized that the problem had never been that Waldo chewed himself. The only problem was ours—we needed to learn how to love a cat properly. Waldo took on the assignment—at some personal sacrifice—and never once gave up on us, until we triumphed. Considering the smell of that ointment, this was no small act of tolerance.

Being a student of human growth, I was impressed by the dramatic results of looking beyond Waldo's neurotic behavior and treating the whole cat with love. I thought of the many people I had helped over the years, and how many of them, in essence, had the habit of chewing at themselves. Isn't that what worry is? What about guilt? Or fear? Low self-esteem? These are obsessive traits by which we gnaw away at our very life vitality. We see each other doing it, but we are so involved in it ourselves that we do not even recognize the horror of it.

Waldo opened my eyes to The Waldo Principle—that the vast majority of human beings go through life chewing away at their own self-image, just as Waldo chewed on his fur. Some of us go to psychiatrists, others go to our pastors for help in changing this condition, but the ointments and medications we are given just refocus the problem. They don't heal it. It will take love—the same kind of love that we give a favorite cat—to heal these neurotic habits. If Waldo could cure himself in one week, given a proper treatment of love, it seems reasonable that most humans ought to be able to do the same within a month—or at least a year.

Years have passed since I learned the Waldo Principle, and Waldo seemed preoccupied primarily with cat pursuits—keeping the household free of mice and chipmunks and safe for democracy. It was to my great surprise, therefore, when I recently discovered that he had been secretly working on, and completed, a manuscript of philosophy. The Wise Cat never actually sleeps, I decided; he is just planning his next lesson for the rest of us.

The manuscript, of course, was not in English—or any other human language. It was in paw prints. At first, I was tempted to ignore the whole thing as random tracks created by Waldo on a muddy spring day. I figured I had left out a ream of paper, and Waldo had run across the sheets with his muddy paws. But as I looked at the papers more carefully— as I was taking them to the trash compacter, I must confess— I realized that there was a pattern, an order, or shall we say a design to them that defied the random muddy footprint theory. I sat down and began to analyze them. Waldo came up and lay down on the papers, as if to confirm that I was on the right track. It did not take me long to realize he had written a collection of stanzas. But actually translating them from the original paw print hieroglyphics into English has taken many long months.

The result is *The Tao of Meow,* the book you are holding

in your hands. It is a collection of 81 verses—nine groups of nine, one for each of a cat's nine lives—in which Waldo reveals his insights into the meaning of life. It is a profound reflection upon life and the way to complete self-fulfillment.

I am well aware that there will be those who will draw a comparison between *The Tao of Meow* and the *Tao Te Ching,* the classic text of the Chinese philosopher Lao Tzu. There are some remarkable parallels, I must admit. Both texts, for instance, contain 81 stanzas. Many of the subjects Waldo deals with are similar to those of Lao Tzu. But I can state unequivocally, without fear of contradiction, that Waldo is not able to read Chinese and probably thinks that Lao Tzu is just a variety of *dim sum*. By the same token, it would not have been possible for Lao Tzu to have read Waldo's manuscript, unless he was the inventor of time travel as well as a great philosopher.

For this reason, I think we must accept the remarkable similarities between the two documents as mere coincidence—the kind of thing that occurs when great minds dwell on the same subjects. It tends to prove to me the unity of the Tao—of which both Lao Tzu and Waldo write—instead of suggesting any kind of copying. Of course, I am sure the great scholars of our age will insist on having the last word on this subject. All I feel obliged to do is offer this remarkable text of Waldo's to the world, for better or for worse.

The text as presented in this book is in its English translation. For the sake of authenticity, however, I am reproducing examples of the text as Waldo wrote it, in the original paw print edition. Each section of nine verses is introduced by one excerpt of this kind from the original. This should be enough to let any scholar verify the accuracy of my translation.

One last note: it should be stated that Waldo agreed to the publication of this book only if his share of the royalties would be donated to fund institutions of higher education for cats of all backgrounds. His wishes will naturally be respected.

Carl Japikse

The Tao of Meow

One

Meow.
If you can utter the one true sound,
You have found the way.
Some humans call the way "the Tao."
All I know is it rhymes with Meow.
And when I say, "Meow," I want my way.
Whether I speak it or not, it is the one true sound,
Because it lets me get my way.

Meow is the beginning of all things,
The source of everything I want.
I don't actually need all things,
Although some humans think *they* do.
Food, shelter, catnip, and mice to catch
Are enough for me.
Although—I will admit—
It's nice to have someone provide these things for me.

I do not know their names—they are the Nameless Ones.
I just call them "Meow."
Meow. They come. They open the door.
I don't know how they do it.
But they do. They know the Meow.

Through the Meow, it is possible to perceive the Subtle.

Through the Meow, it is possible to get what you want.
The Tao of Meow—
The way to get the best of both worlds.

And when I have the best of both,
I lie down on a simple blanket
And contemplate the profound—
Even that which is more profound than the profound,
More subtle than any subtlety—
The purr of perfection
Which is the door to all contentment.

Meow.

Two

Once cats came into being,
It was inevitable that humans would follow.
Everything needs its natural complement,
The emptiness that fills the whole—or is that *hole?*
Good creates the necessity of evil,
Just as surely as difficulty follows ease,
Short follows long, high follows low, front follows back,
And humans respond to my Meow.
These constants never vary.

For this reason,
The Wise Cat spends most of his day asleep.
He knows that if he waits, all things will come to him.
He does not have to set these things in motion,
Just lie in wait until they appear,
Whether it is a mouse or a chipmunk,
Or a Nameless One with dinner.
The Wise Cat is a slave to no thing;
He does what he has to do, but without attachment.
He remains independent.
Humans often think the Wise Cat is aloof,
But what is a *loof?* Just a *fool* spelled backwards.
The Wise Cat is patient.
He lives for himself, not for the things that come to him.
Therefore, he has all things.

Three

I am not just a Wise Cat, but a clever one as well.
I let my people think I am content to sleep in a box,
And so they give me the run of the whole house.
I bring my people the mice I catch,
And so they give me all the food I need to eat.
I show affection to my people only now and then,
And so they shower me with constant affection,
Believing they must win my trust.

This is the Way of the Wise Cat:
Do the opposite of what people expect,
And they will give you what you want.
Just don't tear up their furniture,
Or they will throw you out of the house.

Humans have a mind, but never use it;
The Wise Cat learns to use it for them.
The Tao of Meow is the highest form of simplicity—
If you do the thinking for humans,
They will do your work for you.
They will even tell all their friends
How you have outwitted them,
And everyone will agree that you are "cute."

Four

Once you find the Way, it is not there.
I chased a chipmunk like that once—
It vanished into the fourth dimension.
Is that possible?
It is with the Tao.

Without the Tao,
Your life can be full of emptiness,
Your emptiness can be full of life.
You never need to fill the Tao,
Because it already contains all things—
Not to mention nine lives.

The Tao of Meow lets you land on your feet,
No matter how far you fall;
Lick the burrs from your fur,
Sleep through the glare of the noonday sun,
And cover your personal smells.

Five

Heaven is a Lion; Earth is a Tiger.
I'm just a pussycat. I try to stay out of the fight.
The Wise Cat is content to be who he is;
He does not want to be either Heaven or Earth.
He is able to enjoy the best of both worlds,
Without having to take sides.

Some say there is a vast space between Heaven and Earth.
This may be true,
But it is not my territory.
I know my territory—
I leave the rest to other cats.
I have come to terms with the Tao,
And with the Nameless Ones.
Knowing too much is a good way
To get your whiskers trimmed.
It also suggests that there is a vast space between your ears.

Six

The sun dies every night,
The moon dies every morning.
But the Tao never dies.
It is like a sensuous she-cat.
She-cats go into heat,
They go out of heat,
But their mysterious allure never dies—
Even though I can't quite remember what it is,
Since the Nameless Ones made me a Sexless One.

The Tao is like that. Sexless. Nameless.
It is the root of everything:
Of Heaven and Earth,
Of spirit and form.
Not here or there, and yet everywhere.
It exists simply because most people—and cats—
Fail to see that it exists.
And like a she-cat in heat, it never grows tired.

Seven

The sky is eternal.
Can you imagine life without the sky? Or the stars?
The sky is eternal; eons after you and I
Have vanished into the fourth dimension,
The earth will still be here.
The Tao has a long attention span.
As for me, I can barely wait from snack time to dinner.
But the Tao needs no nourishment.
It has a big belly.

For this reason, the Wise Cat forgets his belly;
The belly of the Tao is large enough to keep him fed.

The Wise Cat makes no claims.
It is not because the Wise Cat is too timid to ask—
He knows the Meow—
It is just that the Tao remembers forever.

When "Meow" is the only word you can utter,
You learn to say what you mean.

Eight

Everything good is like water—
It's a blessing when you need a drink,
But you can drown in too much of it.

As for me, I would rather be stomped on by elephants
Than take a bath.
This is why I know
That the Tao closely resembles water.

It is better to sip the good things of life
Than gulp them.

In hunting, the good is surprise;
In napping, the good is a warm lap.
In running, the good is quickness.
In cunning, the good is wit.
In dining, the good is fullness.
After dinner, the good lies in licking yourself clean.

Either you are part of the Tao, or you are not.
If you are not, don't blame the Tao.
You need to learn to sip life
Without getting in over your head.

Nine

It is good to play with your prey,
But not if it spoils before you eat it.
It is good to inspect your territory on a regular basis,
But not if you miss snack time.
It is easy to be wise,
As long as you don't try to do things
That aren't supposed to be done.

If you pretend to be great,
You will get all of the headaches of greatness,
Without any of the grandeur.
This is not wise.
If you pretend to be powerful,
You will have to defend yourself
Against every half-wit who comes along,
Which makes you a half-wit yourself.

Pretending to be what you are not
Is the best way to fool yourself.

Ten

I look at the stars and want to touch them,
But I can't jump that high.
They are not mine to possess.
I look at the toys scattered around my box;
I can touch these. I play with them all the time.
But they are not mine to possess.
I know they are not mine to possess,
Because when I knock one of them under a dresser,
I cannot retrieve it.
I must wait for a Nameless One to move the dresser
And kick it out,
And that may take months.

My purr of contentment—this is mine;
My tail standing straight up when I swagger—this is mine;
The way I curl round the legs of people—this is mine;
The joy of running at top speed toward the open door
At dinner time—
All this is mine.

It is mine because I express it,
Not because I possess it.
I am an *a priori* kitty.
You scratch my back—or I'll scratch yours.

Eleven

Philosophers have asked,
"If a tree falls in the forest, but no one is there to hear,
Does it make a sound?"
I ask, if a philosopher is sitting in a chair at a desk,
Is it a chair?
Or does it only become a chair when a cat sits in it?
Does paperwork only become important when I lie on it?
For days, it lies on the desk, unmoved;
The moment I lie down on it,
One of the Nameless Ones decides to move it.

This is Virtue;
It has no substance, and yet it exists.
But even though it does exist,
It is nothing until you use it.
In this regard, virtue is very much part of the Meow.
Falling trees, on the other hand, are not.
They make only a thud, not a Meow.
Who would be so foolish as to listen to a thud, anyhow?
Meow.

Twelve

I was lying on my back once,
When a bird flew by overhead.
In one fluid movement, I leaped heavenward.
I think I caught a bit of an angel's wing,
But the bird flew on unmolested.

If you rely on your senses, you can go mad.
Too much light can blind your eyes.
Too much speed can leave you weary.
Too much variety can set you spinning.
Too much cream can make you lose your lunch.

For this reason, in the household of the Wise Cat,
Complexity is an unwelcomed stranger.
The Wise Cat does not try to please the senses;
He dwells instead in virtue,
And waits for the birds to fly lower.

Thirteen

"Honor and dishonor are minted from the same coin."
"Hardship is the door to great opportunity."
These are clichés you can live by.
What do I mean,
"Honor and dishonor are minted from the same coin"?
Honor is not exactly the hottest commodity in town.
If you lose it—watch out!   It will cost you dearly.
If you get it—watch out!   It will cost you even more.
This is why I say it was minted from the coin of dishonor.
Both honor and dishonor can be counterfeit currency.
What do I mean,
"Hardship is the door to great opportunity"?
As any cat knows, doors pose enormous dilemmas.
Should we go out—or stay in?
Should we go in—or stay out?
A hardship is like a kick from a Nameless One—
You don't actually have to make a choice.
Life makes the choice for you,
And kicks you through another door.

If you care enough for me to open the door,
You can trust me with the whole world.
What this has to do with honor and dishonor,
I do not know.
But I am willing to go through the door and find out.

Fourteen

We look and we do not see,
So we assume it isn't there.
We listen and we do not hear,
So we assume it never existed.
We touch but have no feeling—
Yet it never occurs to us that we are the one
Who is numb, dumb, and unaware.

The world is filled with ten thousand things
I can see, hear, and touch.
But it is also filled with uncountable things
That neither you nor I can see, hear, or touch.
None of these things have names,
Yet all of them know the Meow.
They are part of Purrfection.
They are Virtue,
The Cat's Meow.

I am surrounded by the nothing of everything,
The everything of nothing.
It is the form without form,
The image without substance—
The breath without sound.
It arrives before you hear it approaching;
It leaves before you have learned what to do with it.

Some call it Opportunity—
But it is more than Opportunity;
It is Virtue,
A door that swings both ways,
Leading from the beginning to the end and
Back to the beginning.

Meowing will not open the door—
The door is the Meow,
And when it opens,
Life kicks you out to do your business.

Fifteen

I am not the inventor of the Meow,
Just a humble practitioner of its merits.
The Meow has been the Way since time began.

The unknown cat who first discovered the Meow
Was sublime, magical, full of insight.
His understanding cannot be known.
He cannot be known,
And yet, being unknown, we all know him.

Slow to move was he!
Like a cat answering the call of a human.
Uncertain of his goals was he!
He never knew whether to stay in or go out.
Well-tempered and mannered was he!
He hardly ever pulled down the drapes.
True to his nature was he! He was hooked on catnip.
Lost in contemplation was he! He had perfected the catnap.
All-encompassing was he!   He ate far too much.

After the rains, a river cleans itself.
The Wise Cat knows how to clean himself, too—
He is true to his nature.
To utter the Meow, one must be clean;
Otherwise, you may gag on a furball and choke.

Sixteen

Take absurdity to its limit:
It becomes philosophy.

A mountain rises up; ten million years later, it is a valley.
How do I know this?
The empty branch of January, coated with ice and snow,
Is filled with blossoms in May, and fruit in September.
Everything returns to its roots.
This is the basis of serenity—
To know your design and accept it;
To know your fate and embrace it.

If you do not know your design,
You will try to be something you cannot achieve.
If you do not know your fate,
You will become reckless and wild.
This will lead you into danger.

It is my fate to be a ruler of men and women.
I accept this design in all humility.
It is not a destiny I chose; it is part of the Meow.
I am one with the Meow; the Meow is one with me.

I have embraced my fate;
Now, bring me a snack and embrace yours.

Seventeen

There are many kinds of rulers.
The highest rule by virtue; their authority is invisible.
Those they rule are unaware of being ruled.
They may even believe that they are the ones who rule.

The next kind rule by love,
And those they rule praise and honor them.
The next kind rule by fear,
And those they rule become restless, agitated.
The lowest kind rule by muscle,
And those they rule wait for the moment to rebel.

By adhering to these principles,
It is relatively easy for a cat,
Who weighs no more than ten or eleven pounds,
To completely rule a household of four or five humans,
Getting everything he wants,
Giving almost nothing in return.

Rule by terror, and they will take you to a cat shelter.
Rule by fear, and they will give you away
To a family with children.
Rule by love, and they will brag about you;
But if you rule by virtue,
They will believe you to be the best-trained cat in the world.

Eighteen

If you comprehend the Meow,
You have no need for Philosophy.

You know the way,
You do not need to explain it.
How can you explain the way?
Your syllogisms just get in the way.

When you have to explain your actions,
You cannot avoid creating confusion.
When you have to justify your behavior,
You cannot avoid hypocrisy.

From my point of view,
Most *cataclysms*
Have been caused by
Excessive *catechisms*.

Nineteen

There are three basic precepts to wise living.

Eliminate raccoons and possums,
And the fields and gardens will be safe.
Keep the birds at bay,
And the members of your household
Will not want to fly away.
Ban all dogs,
And there will be no terror.

And yet, these rules are not complete.
We must add these principles to them:

Never make a cat wear a collar;
How can you put a leash on the Way?
Never scold a cat for being a "bad kitty";
Unless you are ready to chide the Tao.
And never throw a cat into water,
Unless you want to hear ten thousand variations
On the theme of "Meow,"
Beautifully orchestrated
In less than three seconds.

Twenty

From where I sit, I can see the hill across the way,
And the valley in between.
From where I sit, I can see your point of view,
As you assert the differences between us.
How great is the valley between our two hills?
Can't either one of us walk across this valley?

The one who argues with another
Creates valleys between hills.
Nothing grows in these valleys but weeds.
The one who contends with the Way,
Creates bottomless abysses within himself;
He makes it impossible to journey from hill to hill.
He can utter the Meow,
But all he will hear in return is a dull echo.

The masses are peaceful and quiet;
They have their routines to absorb them.
I can be one with the masses,
For I have my routines as well.
I patrol my territory,
Take a nap,
Have dinner,
Clean myself,
And curl up by one of the Nameless Ones.

But these are the habits of daily activity,
Not the expression of my innermost heart.
My innermost heart listens to the earth.
It may look as though I am sleeping,
But my inner ear is listening,
Listening,
To all that Mother Earth can tell me.

How do I know it is Mother Earth who is speaking?
I know, because I know the Meow.
Besides—she always tells me what I want to hear.
Isn't that what mothers do?

Twenty-One

There are two elements to the Meow.
Me.
And Ow.
Ow and me.
Meow.
This is the nature of the Way—me and ow.
Me! Ow! This contains all images.
Ow! Me! This contains all shapes.
Spoken—or silent. The sound is the same,
Because it is the essence of sound
Which makes the Meow.

From now to never,
The Meow has always been heard—
Beckoning, summoning us
Back to the origin of all things.
How do I know this?
I am Me,
And know enough to avoid the "Ow."

Therefore, I know the Meow.

Twenty-Two

To know Me is to know the Meow.
But do not misconstrue my statement for false vanity.
If I wanted to be vain,
I could do a whole lot better.

He who exaggerates comes up short.
Ow!
He who struts on tall fences falls off.
Ow!
He who shows off will be shown the door.
Ow!
He who brags about his talents will find them tested.
Ow!
He who praises himself generally does so
Only because no one else will volunteer.

Too much of a good thing
Strikes me as just about right.
But too much vanity gives me a belly-ache.

You cannot hear the Meow
If the only things you listen to
Are the echoes of your own conceits.

Twenty-Three

How much truth can a cliché convey?
Clichés are dull, worn out, overused.
Truth is full of light and vigor. It sparkles.
Take the truth and twist it—you get a cliché.
It hides the truth
Behind conundrums, paradoxes, and puzzles.
But then, when you untwist it again,
The truth falls out all over you.
This is the virtue of a twisted mind.

For this reason, the Wise Cat develops a twisted mind—
A mind that can endure
The contortions of logic and rhetoric
And still grasp the simple, whole truth
Within the clichés and contradictions
Of those who think themselves wise.
The Wise Cat claims to know little;
Therefore, he knows much.
The Wise Cat does not strut on railings;
Therefore, he never falls off.
The Wise Cat does not brag;
Therefore, he is thought to be perfect.
The Wise Cat does not praise his own acts;
He knows this is the duty of humans.

When you have a twisted mind,
You never have to worry
About people misunderstanding you—
It goes without saying.
You will never be accused of being dull,
Because you will always be coming up with a new twist!

If this doesn't make sense,
Don't blame me.
It's just your own twisted mind that is confusing you.
I know exactly what I am saying.
It's up to you to untwist your own preconceptions,
If you hope to understand
These brilliant truths.
Meow.

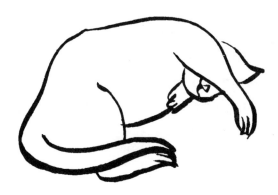

Twenty-Four

The Meow is never shrill;
It is never shouted.
It is spoken gently, quietly—often silently.
It takes a well-tuned ear to hear a Meow
That makes no sound.

No one actually speaks the Meow.
Who would the Speaker be?
Is it not enough that Nature can speak the Meow?
If all of us were speaking the Meow,
How could any one of us hear it?

The Meow is the Word that never passes lips;
It is something we become, rather than utter.
If you become the Meow,
You will find the Tao,
You will be shown the Way.
If you become Virtue, you will know that Virtue.
If you stay the way you are, that's your own tough luck.
Don't come bellyaching about it to me.
I only have ears for Meow.

Twenty-Five

All was still—then the stillness was broken.
It is the Meow that broke the stillness.
Before Heaven and Earth were, the Meow was heard.
Soft and gentle! Unchanging and profound!
The voice that called Heaven and Earth into being.
I do not know its name: I call it the "Meow."
If I had to give it a second name,
I would call it "The Supreme."

"Meow" rhymes with "Tao";
"Supreme" rhymes with "cream";
Cream rises to the top,
And there you find the Tao.

The Meow is Supreme,
Heaven's a dream,
Earth is mighty—
And the Wise Cat always tries to cooperate
With the powers that be.

For this reason, look for your joy on earth,
For the earth looks for its joy in heaven;
Heaven finds its joy in the Way,
And the Way finds its joy in being.
I, of course, find my joy in cream—as often as I can.

Twenty-Six

It is gravity that permits levitation,
Just as it is serenity that masters irritation.

For this reason, a seasoned traveler has learned
Never to check his baggage,
If he expects to have it at the end of the flight.
You should not expect to take it with you,
Unless it will fit under the seat in front of you.

If you disregard this sage advice,
You will discover the law of gravity;
If you let yourself become agitated,
The size of your tail will give you away.

Twenty-Seven

It is good to run through a woods
Without making a sound.
It is good to let your friends know your thoughts
Without betraying them to your enemies.
It is good to know which door to go to
When you want back in the house.
It is good to know where
The mice and the chipmunks will build their nests.
It is good to know when a storm is brewing,
So you can stay inside.

The Wise Cat is good at all he attempts,
Knowing that if he does not make the attempt,
This is bad.
But even the bad becomes the basis
For attempting the good,
When it becomes so bad you can
No longer stand the aroma.

Not everyone comprehends the Way.
Some are confused.
They believe in right and wrong,
But think the one excludes the other.
Therefore, they are confused.
I believe in right and wrong,

But having tasted bad cream,
I know they often come together.
Therefore, I am not confused.
Rightness is the ultimate conclusion of wrongness,
Once it tires of being wrong,
Just as a nap is the crowning achievement of activity,
Once it tires of being awake.
Yogurt, on the other hand, is a complete waste of time—
Like a six-legged cow.

51

Twenty-Eight

When you can be both right and wrong at the same time,
Then you can become an open meadow
In which enemies meet and reconcile their differences.
You will be known as one of redeeming virtue,
And this virtue will sustain you.
School children will be forced to memorize your name.

When you can be pure of thought,
Yet practical at the same time,
Then you will become a river filled with melting snows.
You will nurture the community in which you live,
And this virtue will sustain you.
Pigeons will flock to the statues they build in your honor.

I prefer a more innocuous form of virtue,
One of being both here and there at the same time.
It is easy to be both right and wrong;
It is sensible to be both idealistic and pragmatic;
But it takes a sheer magician
To be both here and there at the same time.

Here—in the flesh and blood.
There—with only my Cheshire smile remaining.
When here is not good enough, there will have to do.
When there tires of me, suddenly I reawaken here.

Here, there. Then, now.
I want them both,
Without having to divide my allegiances.
This is the glory of the Tao—
If you cannot hear me Meow in this world,
You better believe you will hear me in the next.

It is not that I am confused;
Neither is the Tao.
If anything seems confusing,
It must be that you have fallen into a time warp—
Perhaps by trying to split the here and now.

Try to remember:
The Meow of the Tao
Is the Tao of Meow.

Twenty-Nine

It is foolish to want to dominate the world;
It is an ambition which simply cannot succeed.
To dominate the world
Would necessitate crushing the Tao.
But the Meow is sacred;
It cannot be hushed.
Nor can it be perverted to ambitious ends.

Those who would control the Meow
End up destroyed;
Those who would hold onto the Meow
End up losing everything.

There are those who believe that they own things;
Some people believe that they own cats—
Or other humans.
These people do not even own themselves.

It may be possible to own a clock,
But no one can own Time.
It may be possible to own a garden,
But no one can make the sun shine on it.
It may be possible to control great wealth—
But what is wealth to a pussycat?
A newly discovered nest of mice.

And when wealth is gone, it is gone,
Unless you have tapped the Mother lode of the Tao.

Therefore,
The Wise Cat rejects ambition, domination, and greed.
He is well pleased to enjoy
The abundance of mice and chipmunks
The Tao provides,
And give thanks to the Great Meow.

Thirty

Only he who rules himself can rule others.
Would you use a gun or a bomb to force yourself
To do something you did not want to do?
Of course not. Nor can others be forced in this way.

The good hunter catches his prey and is well satisfied.
He does not use the occasion
To fill the other mice and chipmunks with fear,
Lest they leave the area and go somewhere else.
He catches his prey but does not become cocky;
He may play with it, of course,
But this is just his way of expressing thanks to the Tao.

For he knows that unless the Tao had created his prey,
It would not be there for him to catch,
And he would die of great hunger.
Without the Tao, the hunter is helpless—
Unless, of course, there is a friendly human to feed him;
But this, too, is part of the Tao.

When you take the abundance of life for granted,
This is called "The short road to nowhere."
Do not take this road,
Lest the Tao begin to take *you* for granted,
And show you precisely where the road ends.

Thirty-One

Everything has its natural prey.
This is part of the Meow—part of the Way.
But when one kills, it must be to honor the Way—
To sustain life—
Not to defy the Way, and prove yourself superior.

To kill a mouse, I must be at one with the Meow,
At one with the Way.
But I know that the mouse is also one with the Way.
This is why he has come my way,
And I have come his way.
There is no other way.
So I kill him. He's in the way.

When you must kill a mouse, or any living creature,
Do not think of it as something to boast about.
Neither should you shrink from it and be squeamish.
Remain calm and serene,
Knowing that it is the Way in you meeting the Way in it.
And thus you send it on its way.

If you take delight in killing,
You are not at one with the Way.
If you take delight in winning,
You can have no idea what you have lost.

Anyone who wins simultaneously loses,
Just as anyone who loses simultaneously gains.
This is the balance of life.
The one who knows the Way is in balance,
And expresses balance in all he does,
Even killing.

I kill when I must.
I am merely grateful
That my natural prey consists of mice and chipmunks—
And not hippopotamuses.
Such is the virtue of balance.

Thirty-Two

I call the Tao the Meow,
Because it is forever nameless.
No one owns it;
It is not Waldo's Way
Or Kant's Way
Or the Pythagorean Theorem.
It is not even the highway, the byway, or the freeway.
It is just the way, the sound of the Meow.
No one can see it or own it,
Yet no one dares to claim it.
If you could embrace it, you would instantly disappear,
And never again reappear,
Except when the mist hangs low in the valley.

Do not try to name the Way,
Be content with the Meow.
If you give it a name,
You will reduce it to a *thing,*
And the Way is not a thing—it is the source of all things.
You might as well try to name each raindrop,
Pretending that only the drops exist,
And there is no such thing as rain.

Be content to know the Meow,
And be glad that you are not all wet.

Thirty-Three

To see the Way in others is the first step to wisdom.
To see the Way in yourself is an omen of good to come.
To rule by invoking the Way within others
Takes you many miles.
To let the Way rule yourself completes the journey.

To know that the Way satisfies your needs
Is the first step to wealth.
To persevere in meeting your goals is an omen of spring.
To sustain your efforts no matter the obstacle
Will give you good fortune.

And if you can take it with you when you die,
You have truly found the Way.

Thirty-Four

The Meow can be heard everywhere,
Floating through the trees on a summer eve,
Or echoing from the depths of a canyon.

It is to the left, if you are right-handed;
It is to the right, if you are left-handed.
If you are ambidexterous,
Then you know how to go both ways at once.

It achieves what it sets forth to achieve.
Everything depends on it, yet nothing is enslaved to it.
Everything comes from it, yet everything returns to it.
It is just as much alive in the tiniest mosquito
As it is in the mammoth behemoth.

It has no name, yet lives in every name.

For this reason,
The capacity of a Wise Cat to accomplish great things
Depends on his ability
To be content with whatever he has;
I need almost nothing at all—
Just a Nameless One to take care of me—
Which is why I am a Wise Cat.

Thirty-Five

When you feel your grip on things slipping,
Let them slip.
Remain steady in the Meow,
And the whole world will come to you.

Good food, strong drink, and shelter—
For these things travelers stop.
But only the wise will stop to listen to the Meow.
It seems so unimportant.
When you look at it, there is nothing to see.
When you listen for it, there is nothing to hear.

And yet, it does have its virtue:
The Meow is the one thing in life
No government has ever been able to tax.

Thirty-Six

Before you can shrink it, you must first stretch it.
Before you can weaken it, you must first reinforce it.
Before you can discard it, you must first embrace it.
Before you can diminish it, you must first enrich it.

This is the Strategy of the Way:
In order to triumph, you must surrender;
In order to rule, you must submit.

The birds that feed by the window
Trust in a pane of glass.
They do not realize that in springtime
The window will be opened.

Thirty-Seven

The Tao has a life of its own;
It is not like a public relations campaign
Sponsored by the Chamber of Commerce.
Politicians cannot control it.
Special interests groups cannot lobby it.
You and I cannot vote on it.

If you try to make it complex, it will confuse you.
Complexity is the armor of desire;
If you are without desire, you can know the Way.

When I sound the Meow,
I can have my way,
But only because I do not need it or want it.
You can learn to do the same.

And if you do,
Then everything you do
In Heaven or on Earth
Will be correct and right—
Unless, of course, you happen to get in *my* way.

Thirty - Eight

When it comes to cats,
The highest virtue is to have no burrs in your coat.
The loss of virtue is therefore a painful experience—
Have you ever tried to remove burrs with your tongue?

A cat with great virtue can walk through a field of burrs
And come out with a clean coat.
A cat without virtue will return from the same field
With enough burrs to carpet your floor.

If you are a cat without superior virtue,
It is a good idea to have a Nameless One close by,
To pick out your burrs.
It gives you a level of virtue you do not deserve—
And makes the Nameless One feel good.

Lose your burrs and you gain virtue.
Lose your virtue and you will surely gain burrs.
There would be little virtue in this world,
If there were no combs and brushes,
And Nameless Ones to use them.

Therefore, always remember—
When the Way is lost,
You still have your virtue,

Unless you have burrs,
In which case you still have humanity
To take care of you.

It is not a question of whether your hair is thick or thin,
Or whether it is the season for burrs or not.
These are universal rules all cats must live by.
It does not matter if you accept them or reject them;
Virtue is not a state of mind—
It is a state of burr-less-ness,
A state in which you are one with the Meow,
And know the hard core of reality.

It's a state in which you may suddenly realize
That this whole treatise is just a burlesque—
The highest state of Meow.

Thirty - Nine

Being one with the Meow—
The skies are clear, the earth is firm,
The angels, divine;
Valleys are low, and mountains are high.

Skies without clarity would be cloudy.
The earth without firmness would be squishy.
The angels, without divinity, would be dogs.
The valleys, without lowness, would be plains,
As would the mountains, without highness.
So you can see the advantage of being
At one with the Meow.

The high has its base in the low,
The low puts its hope in the high—
This is why I am called a Wise Cat
And why humans are known as "The Nameless Ones."
It's not that they are lacking names—
It's just that they put too much stock in them.

They also put too much stock in their cars,
Their houses, and the clothes they wear.
They would be much richer if they had none of this stuff,
But knew who they were,
And knew the Meow.

Forty

If you hold a mirror to the Meow,
You will understand it.
If you hold a mirror to my face,
You will see a gorgeous Puss.

The problem with holding a mirror to the Meow,
Is finding the Meow in the first place.
Philosophically speaking, it has no "first place";
It is everywhere and no where, all at the same time.

Do not let this trouble you, however;
Find me and you find the Meow;
Serve me and you serve the Meow.

Being a Wise Cat,
This is the least I can do for you.

Forty - One

I have an important distinction to make.
Many people hear the Call.
This is not the same as the Way.

The Call is something like a speeding ticket—
It is the voice of God telling you to shape up.
But people who hear the Call
Usually fail to get the message.
They think they must be someone important
To have heard the voice of God,
So they become Evangelists.

This is like the story of the fellow who told everyone
That he was on a special mission from the King,
Doing the work of the King, as directed by the King.
It was not a lie, either. It's just that no one asked,
What the King had actually said.
In my book, it is not much of a Call to be told,
"Get out of my way!"

When you hear the Call, therefore, remember—
You are being summoned to find the Way,
Not go around boasting that you already know it.
If you hear the call, it is time to change your ways—
Not lecture everyone else.

The Way is different.
It is at its brightest when it appears to be dark.
If you seem to be going forward
It's a good bet you're going backwards.
If the journey is rough, things are going smoothly.
The highest virtue will soon be tarnished,
And the weakest will end up with the most strength.
The only stability is to be found in change.

The Way takes you into dimensions
Where squares have no corners,
Perfection is always outdoing itself,
You can't tell a cat from a dog,
And the Meow has no beginning or ending.

If you have heard the Meow,
The last thing you would do is become an Evangelist.
My guess is—you would become a cat.

Forty - Two

Originally, there was nothing in the Way.
Then, something got in the Way;
The Divine Cat meowed, and all things were born.

All things are both male and female,
Which is why there is so much confusion in the world.
I, on the other hand, have been neutered,
Which is probably what makes me so wise.

Everyone hates to be homeless, hungry, and alone,
Yet everyone spends most of each day
In these conditions,
Without a second thought.
When I patrol my boundaries, I am homeless,
Although my home is there when I return.
When I am in between meals, I am hungry,
Although I can always wheedle a snack from a human.
When I am by myself, I am alone,
Even though somewhere a lap is calling my name.

For this reason,
It does not matter whether we are knaves or kings—
We are all homeless, hungry, and alone
Unless we know the Meow,
By which all things are born.

Forty - Three

Which is stronger—
A swamp or a boulder of granite?
The granite seems stronger,
But toss it into the swamp,
And it will disappear without a trace in the muck.

Which is better—
Doing good or taking a nap?
If you do good, you will exhaust your strength,
And collapse into a deep fog of sleep.
You should have taken the nap in the first place—
Then you would still have your strength.

I believe in serving the world by taking naps;
Many people have concurred
That this is the best way I can be of help.
In my opinion, most people who try to do good
Probably ought to be taking naps, too.

Forty - Four

I have watched humans haul great loads back and forth,
And have to pause to sweat and pant.
The only things I ever carry are chipmunk and mice,
And they have never caused me to lose my breath.

Humans also carry great loads of worry, fear, and desire,
Back and forth, back and forth.
It makes them sweat and wheeze,
And sometimes wet their pants.
I carry no burden, since everything I need
I can find along the Way,
By sounding the Meow.

If you are pleased with what life gives you,
You will always be contented;
If you know when to pause,
You need never sweat or wheeze.
Unless, of course,
Some dumb human sticks you in a small cage
When the temperature outside is about one hundred.

Forty - Five

Too much confusion seems misleading,
But its clarity is never found.
Too much moderation seems excessive,
Yet it serves limited circumstances well.

I love these paradoxes, don't you?

A straight line may well be crooked,
Depending upon the angle of your perspective.
A sensible philosophy may well be absurd,
When applied to the actual context of daily life.

This is why I prefer naps to great activity;
There is good reason to believe
That actual involvement in daily life
Would ripple the waters of my serene idleness.

It would be terrible to discover
That I am not as wise as I thought I was.

Forty - Six

When the world is at one with the Meow,
The streets are filled with gentle laughter.
When the world is at odds with the Meow,
The streets are filled with discord and fights.

In either event, I try to stay out of the streets,
Lest I become one with a speeding automobile,
And utter my ultimate Meow.
The Wise Cat knows his limits,
And does not transcend them,
Lest he should be transformed into a human.

Forty - Seven

You can know the whole world
Without leaving your home.
You can find the Way of the Meow,
Without crossing your threshold.

One may journey to the ends of the earth
And never find them,
Because there is no end to the endless,
As you are doubtless beginning to realize.

Therefore, the Wise Cat pursues the Way
Without giving the Way cause to pursue him.
He acts by doing nothing;
He moves forward by going nowhere.

This is all well and good,
Unless you have left loose ends
In your quest for the endless.

Forty - Eight

"Smile, and the whole world smiles with you."
Meow, and the whole world purrs.
But those who do not know the Meow,
Cannot meow along with you.
They are not in tune with the Way.
Their smiles are more forced and strained;
They try to make the natural artificial.
When you smile because you are part of the Way,
It is as though you are not smiling at all.
It takes no effort.
Your joy increases,
Even while the effort it takes to smile decreases.

Eventually, the effort to act ceases altogether.
You look in the mirror, and there is nothing there,
Except the grin of a Cheshire cat.
This is all that is left of you—
The rest belongs to the Meow.

Forty - Nine

The Wise Cat never limits himself, even to nine lives.
If I need more than nine lives,
Why restrict myself in this way?
You have to watch people, though;
They will restrict you in all kinds of ways,
And threaten to chalk off one of those nine lives,
If you do not do as they request.

"Don't scratch the woodwork," they shout;
"Use your scratching post."
But why should I use my scratching post,
Which is in another room,
When the door jamb will do just as well?
Haven't I just expounded on the virtue of inaction?
Don't they know the Way?
Humans simply do not have an open mind,
Nor understand the need of the Wise Cat to scratch.

It's a simple matter of trust.
I trust them to feed me in the morning and at night,
And dry me when I come in sopping wet from the rain.
They should trust me to know where to scratch—
And I certainly think I know it better than they!
How can people hope to evolve,
When they are so backwards and fixed in their thoughts?

Fifty

If a cat has nine lives,
Does he have nine deaths as well?

Some people think no one knows what death is like,
But that is ridiculous.
I know, because I am a Wise Cat.
I know, because the Meow knows,
And I am part of the Meow.

Death is just life in reverse;
You step out of life into death,
You step out of death into life.
Death is a lover we keep on trying to leave,
But somehow never manage to forget.

Some people are afraid of death,
Yet they live so stupidly
That their life is constantly slipping away from them.
They are like a sieve,
So full of holes that the life force leaks right out of them.
It leaks through their fears,
Their worries,
And their lusts;
It leaks through their wishes,
Their dreams,

And their faults.
They start dying the moment they are born.

The Wise Cat cherishes the life force within him
And does not let it leak away.
He acts with trust, courage, kindness, patience, and joy,
So there is no place for his life force to slip out.
When death does come,
It arrives in a carriage with four horses,
So that he can make a proper exit from this world,
And never be accused of cheating death.

The Wise Cat lands in the Afterworld
On all four paws.

Fifty - One

We are all born of the Meow,
Which may come as a shock to some of our Mothers,
Although they can testify to the "Ow."

It is Virtue, however, that nurtures us.
As for me, I prefer the kind of Virtue
That comes in those little cans—
Although an occasional mouse makes a nice snack.

Born of the Way,
Nurtured by Virtue,
Shoved around by Fate—
Whose life is this, anyway?
Who picks up the tab?

There is only one answer: the Meow.
But there are a number of rules. To wit:
Do not cheat the Way—
It charges a very high interest on overdue accounts.
Do not run away from Virtue—
It will mug you in a dark alley.
Do not get into a shoving match with Fate—
It will knee you in the groin.

These are Waldo's rules for sane living.

Fifty - Two

The world was also born of the Meow—
A phenomenon almost too great
For even a Wise Cat to imagine.

At times, even now, when I feel insecure,
I will crawl up on the bed of a sleeping Nameless One
And knead the blankets with my paws,
Just as I did when I was a suckling kitten.
I do that even though I know I was born of the Meow.

If the world was born of the Meow as well—
Whose bed does it crawl into when it needs comforting?
Where does it turn for security?

You can close your eyes and see truth.
You can open your eyes and see falsehood.
It is not what your eyes see that counts;
It is what your mind understands.

Philosophers tell us the world emerged out of nothing—
A vast primordial Stillness.
But if the world was born of stillness,
Then it must have been stillborn.

Or maybe that just applies to Philosophy.

Fifty - Three

There are many different roads in life.
Some are built by humans.
These are not safe for cats,
Lest you end up being memorialized by a bumper sticker.

Some are made by cats,
As we patrol our territory.
If humans try to follow these roads,
They will end up stuck in briars.

Then there is the road of Life.
It is very level and easy to follow,
Even if you do not know where you are going.
In spite of this,
Many of us prefer to make our own roads.

This is the source of dead ends and frustration;
It is the source of fantasy and unfulfilled wishes.
It is the source of manipulation and exaggeration—
Not to mention never-ending circles.

If you end up in the same spot,
Day after day,
You can be pretty sure
You are not following the Way.

Fifty - Four

When you jump from a high ledge,
It is a good idea to land upright, on all four legs.
This may require making adjustments in mid flight.

It is Virtue that lets you make these adjustments,
Not just in jumping from ledges,
But also in the way you deal with others,
In your hopes and expectations,
In the goals you set for achievement,
And in the way you treat life.

If you can end up standing upright,
With all four legs on the ground,
In everything you undertake to do,
Then you know Virtue, and Virtue knows you.

If, on the other hand, you tend to get run over
By the steamroller of life,
You probably do not yet know everything
You need to learn.

Fifty - Five

The newborn kitten knows nothing,
Must learn everything.
This is a good attitude for the Wise Cat, too.
The moment we assume we know something,
Even our own territory,
We cease to be wise—
For who knows what changes have occurred,
Since the last time we patrolled it?

I am a small cat.
How could I hope to embrace all of wisdom,
So that I would know everything there is to know?
It can embrace me, but I can never hope to embrace it.
I might as well believe
I can catch every mouse in the field!
What vanity! What arrogance!
As long as mice are part of the Way,
And are embraced by the Way,
How could I be so foolish as to presume
That I could catch and eat them all?

Such ambition is not part of "the Meow."
It is more apt to be part of a colossal case of heartburn.
It also suggests that you need to go on a diet.

Fifty - Six

There is something greater than Virtue;
It is that which gives rise to Virtue.
You cannot know it from your ordinary pursuits;
You can only know it in moments of pure intimacy.

For the sake of any prudes who might read this,
I should distinguish between "being in heat"
And pure intimacy.
Being in heat drives you insane;
Pure intimacy merely drives you in—
In to the absolute wholeness of your being.

So shutter the windows, lock the door,
Turn down the light, and take the phone off the hook.
It is time to experience the ultimate experience,
Which is not even an experience,
Because it does not happen.
Pure intimacy.

You can't buy it; I can't sell it.
You can't seize it; I can't defend it.
You can't debase it, because you can't find it—
It drives you up the old screen door, doesn't it?

I guess it is like being in heat, after all.

Fifty - Seven

Be upright and dignified in patrolling your territory;
Be cunning and shifty when catching mice.
The rest of the time, do as little as you can,
Let humans provide you with what you need.

Humans are a species of life, too.
They have their role to play.
Many times, they take these roles so seriously—
Buying and selling,
Building and destroying,
Judging and misjudging—
That they estrange themselves from the Way.
They forget their purpose in living,
Which is to provide for the comfort of cats.

The Wise Human therefore knows:
It is better to do nothing at all,
Than to forget to take care of cats.
Give cats a warm home,
And you will have tranquillity.
Give cats whatever they desire to eat,
And you will be blessed with abundance.
Make cats the first cause in your life,
And you will understand the Meow.

Fifty - Eight

When humans are confused,
It is easy to manipulate them.
When they are self-absorbed,
They won't even hear you meow.

Good and bad fortune arrive on the same ship.
What seems to be good often is bad;
What seems to be bad often is good.
This is also true of Philosophy.

Just because something has been quoted
For three thousand years
Does not mean there is any wisdom in it.
People can be bewildered for a very long time.
Cats can stay confused for nine lives.

To become wise, you must solve the riddles of life.
To be wise, you must forget the riddles of life.
Then nothing will confuse you—
Although it is a good idea to keep this fact to yourself.

Fifty - Nine

I went on a diet once.
It's not what everyone makes it out to be.
I lost a few pounds,
But I have since regained them.
What did I learn?

If you are going to go on a diet, do it sensibly.
Eat all the chocolate and cream that you want,
But stay away from anger and fear,
Jealousy and malice,
Irritation and grief.
These are all things that weigh us down;
These are the excess pounds we need to lose.

Once you truly lose them,
You won't regain them.
A burden is lifted; you become as light as a feather,
Able to float up into the very essence of your being.

That which you try to possess will control you.
The only way to control something is to forego it.
I therefore have all the chocolate and cream in the world,
When I refrain from eating them.
I just don't ask the scale for confirmation.

Sixty

Leading others is like throwing darts.
It's only humiliating if you miss the board entirely.

If you hit the bulls-eye,
You are in tune with the Meow.
No matter how good your opponents are,
They are no match for you.

This is true in all cases but one—
If the bull's eye is not on a dartboard,
But between a bull's ear.
Then you had better run like hell.

Sixty - One

Cats are superior to humans,
Because cats let humans think they have made us pets.

Dogs make pets; hamsters make pets;
Cats only go through the motions.
They may seem to submit to being a pet,
But it is only to give humans a chance to learn how
To provide cats with the comforts they require.

The one thing about humans is their ego;
It is important for them to feel that they are dominant.
The best way to control them, therefore,
Is to appear to submit to their commands.

Then, once they are convinced that they are in control,
You can break any of the rules—
In fact, do just about anything—
And the smug human will not mind.
He will probably even praise you
For following his commands so well.

Sixty - Two

Everything has its price,
Including me.
I can be bought.

Not with expensive toys or gourmet delicacies—
I am a "fish and chips" cat, myself—
Or with all of the money in the world.
I said I could be bought, not bribed.

The Way is the treasure of the Wise Cat.
Add to my treasure, and I will trust you
In all endeavours.
Help me learn to perceive the Meow more clearly,
And I will follow you to the ends of the earth.

I can be bought,
But my price is greater
Than that of any king.
I am prepared, however, to give very attractive terms:
The debt can be amortized over the whole of eternity.

Editor's Note: In Waldo's manner of speaking, "fish & chips" means shrimp cocktail (hold the sauce) and chipmunks.

Sixty - Three

You cannot move mountains,
If you believe them to be mountains.
You must think of them as collections of small stones,
Which can be moved one at a time,
And then reassembled.

Make work difficult, and it cannot be done.
Make it simple, and even a simpleton can do it.
There is great virtue in hard work,
As long as someone else is doing it.

Sixty - Four

Never kill a mouse or chipmunk
Who is a mother-to-be;
If you do, you are making your own work
So much more difficult!
Follow the mouse back to her nest
And wait for her to give birth to her brood.
Then, as they grow older,
You can pick them off one by one,
Generation after generation,
With virtually no effort.

This is the way of the Meow;
If you understand first principles,
You can attain anything you want,
With almost no effort whatever.

Of course, if the mice and chippies
Understood first principles,
They would probably move out of the neighborhood.
This confirms the old adage,
"A little knowledge is a dang'rous thing."

Sixty - Five

It is not necessary to be clever
In order to know the Meow.
In fact, cleverness can be a distinct disadvantage.

Cleverness is a game played in shallow water,
A competition between two players,
Both of whom ultimately lose.
Wisdom is a deep well of insight to be shared by all.

If you rely on cleverness alone,
You will be in big trouble;
When a drought strikes,
There will be no creek to paddle your canoe in.

The individual who tries to outsmart everyone else,
Usually ends up outsmarting himself.
His attempts to fool the Way
Rebound
And expose the fool within himself.
It is never clever to be a fool,
Although it is generally foolish to be clever.

Cats are often thought to be clever,
Because we outwit humans so constantly.
This is no great test of either cleverness or foolishness.

Sixty - Six

Nameless Ones do not know very much about the Meow.
They do so many strange things!

They buy and sell.
What does this mean?
How can anyone own a part of the Meow—
Let alone a piece of the rock?
They try to buy low and sell high,
But they aren't very good at it—
They all seem to be in debt.

We are all in debt to the Way, of course,
But the Nameless Ones do not understand this.
They think they are in debt to banks, and credit unions,
And one another.
They think they own things,
And yet most of them do not even own themselves.
They think they own cats—
Now, there's a role reversal!

There's another strange thing about humans, too.
They desperately want to be led.
Where, I have not yet figured out.
Or why, for that matter.
Cats like to be independent,

But humans crave to be led.
So they elect leaders,
But the leaders are not really interested in leading—
They want power.
They want to be acclaimed as "great."
They want to go down in history.

Not a one of them knows anything of the Way.
If they did, they would study the Meow
And learn to utter the Meow,
So they could lead their followers along the Way.

It is my humble observation
That leaders who go down in history,
Take most of their generation with them.

Therefore, if you wish to step into the future,
Follow the Way.
If you wish to go down in history
Follow a leader.
Just remember—
You may go further down than you had counted on.

Sixty - Seven

If the world acclaims you as Great,
Take my advice and duck.
Even if you know the Meow and are one with it,
Do not presume to be Great.
The true meaning of the word "great"
Is "popular target."

I do not need to be great, because I have three treasures.
The first is charm;
The second is wit;
The third is the ability to refrain from using the first two.

Because of my charm, I can be firm.
Because of my wit, I do not mind appearing foolish.
And, because I can refrain from using my charm and wit,
I am a delightful cat to be around.

If you try to be firm without charm,
People will dislike you;
If you are foolish without the wit to appear wise,
People will disdain you.
If you force your charm and wit on others,
They will regard you as a pain in the neck—
A *great* pain in the neck.
This is why it is not a good idea to be great.

Sixty - Eight

If you are a good hunter,
Do not advertise this fact to the mice,
Or they will leave the area.
If you are a great Tom,
Do not boast of this to the other male cats,
Or they will constantly put you to the test.
If you are a good leader,
Devote yourself to following the Way,
So that you will not have to stop and ask directions,
Halfway to your destination.

Be content to let greatness be great:
Have the common sense to be common.

Sixty - Nine

I do not understand why humans
Are so fascinated with strategies and war.
I can understand fighting for a tasty chipmunk,
But I cannot understand fighting for power.

Power is a part of the Meow,
It is there for all.
Only the fool would ever fight for it,
For the more you fight for it,
The less you will have.

Power comes from understanding,
Not from fighting.
You may be able to kill me,
But you cannot kill the Meow.
It will live forever,
As will my charm, my wit,
And my determination not to impose them on you.

For this reason, it can be written
That the one who triumphs in war, loses.
After all, he has vanquished only himself.

Seventy

The Way is easy to understand,
And even easier to follow.
This is why almost no one in the world understands it,
And even fewer follow it.

That makes perfectly good sense, doesn't it?

If the Way was something I could bottle,
And put up for sale,
Everyone would want it.
I would become a very rich cat.

But the Meow cannot be sold,
Although I, personally, do have a price.
Nor can the Meow be stolen,
Or even bought on layaway.

It is therefore something everyone ignores,
Except the few that have come to treasure it.
That suits me fine.
If you are content with your crumbs of glory,
I'll try to be satisfied
With my diamonds and opals of truth.

Seventy - One

If you know you know nothing, you know.
If you know not that you know nothing, you don't know.
If you do, you don't;
If you don't, you do—
Is this philosophy,
Or a primer for two year olds trying to learn to speak?

Seventy - Two

Respect the realities of life.
Do not try to squeeze two people through
A space too small for even one to pass.
Do not force an animal into a corner
Where it must defend itself.
When you meet resistance, understand it.
It is part of the Way.
Take it in stride, and you can find the way around it.

If for some reason you cannot find
Your way around it,
Then do what I do—
Slip into the fourth dimension
And have a nice catnap.

Seventy - Three

Humans make carpets to walk on;
Sometimes they even fantasize flying on them.
The cat knows the true purpose of rugs—
We lie under them.

First you slip one paw under the fringe,
And lift the edge of the carpet up;
Then you scoot quickly underneath,
So that the rug covers your whole body,
Except the tail,
Which is probably sticking out from underneath,
Wagging back and forth as you lie and wait in hiding.

You may think this is an idle game,
But we know that a carpet is the fabric of life.
Either you cloak yourself in it,
Or you strive against it.

Only the foolish tread on the fabric of life.
The wise crawl underneath and become one with it.

Seventy - Four

When a cat senses that a storm is brewing,
He knows it is time to go indoors.
It is not fear that drives him to seek shelter;
It is knowledge.

People do not seem to have this knowledge.
They build their homes by the edge of a river,
Then act surprised when it is flooded in the spring.

Lacking an understanding of the Way,
People fill themselves with fear.
Living in fear,
They can be easily frightened—even by a mouse.

A mouse! Can you imagine it?
I could understand a mouse
Being frightened by a human,
But a human frightened by a mouse?
No wonder they cower and let their leaders
Take away their freedoms and replace them with fear.

These are the same people
Who call us "scaredy cats."

There's never a mirror handy when you need one.

Seventy - Five

It has taken cats thousands of years
To domesticate humans properly.
Even today, the work is not yet complete.
In some rural areas, for instance,
People still exclude cats from their homes.
These people have not yet heard the Meow.

There are even people who do not like cats.
These are people without joy, without light.
They carry themselves through life
Like a heavy burden,
Trodding, plodding, they move from birth to death,
Without discovering the secret of life.

These are the truly poor,
The poor of heart who must be pitied.
They starve in the midst of plenty;
They grovel when they should stand tall;
They die even though they are alive.

Those who enjoy life,
Love cats.
This is the Way—
The heart of virtue.

Seventy - Six

If you love cats,
And pamper me,
I will wrap my tail around your leg,
And share the way of the Meow with you.
I might even nip your knee.
At night, I will curl up with you on your lap,
And you will be comforted by my soft, warm, supple
Body of fur.

If you dislike cats,
Or mistreat me,
It will be very difficult for me
To recognize the living essence within you.
I will probably mistake you for a dead stump,
And use you for a scratching post.

This is why we say
The Way
Is soft, warm, and supple.

Seventy - Seven

I finished this book a dozen verses ago,
But didn't know when to stop.
If I had known when to stop,
And had actually stopped,
This would not have made
A very good book on Philosophy.
Philosophers never stop when they ought to.
They are afraid the reader has failed to grasp
Their sublime message,
So they keep on hammering away at it,
Until the point has become thoroughly dull.
They repeat themselves until everyone stops listening.

This is not the Way;
The Way does not ramble on excessively;
It gets to the point and then quits.
So why am I still going on?
I may have reached the Way,
But you haven't.
You are, however, getting close—
To the End, if not the Way.

Seventy - Eight

There is one thing I have never understood—
Why do humans constantly blame each other
For the mistakes and unpleasantries of life?

If there are three cats in a room,
And an expensive vase happens to fall off a table
And crash into tiny bits on the floor,
We do not sit there,
Waiting for a human to arrive on the scene,
And then point our paws at one another, saying,
"Don't look at me, he did it—
I was just enjoying a cat nap."

I should say not!
We all leave as quickly as we can,
And only return when the coast is clear.

Humans are possessed with the idea of blame.
And yet, it is clear to me,
As it would be to anyone in tune with the Way,
That the vase was no longer needed in this life.
It had outlived its usefulness—
It was in the Way.
So the Way knocked it out of the Way,
Possibly with the help of a swishing tail.

Why blame a cat for an act of Nature?
Why blame each other
For the mistakes and accidents of Life?

It's over and done with;
Let's not shed any tears over
The broken shards of life.

Seventy - Nine

If you would win your point,
Be prepared to give in.
The one who can win gracefully is even more powerful
Than the one who can lose gracefully.

Above all, do not hold grudges and resentments.
Resentments punish no one more severely
Than the one who carries them.
You cannot carry a grudge
And act gracefully at the same time.

Learn this lesson from a Wise Cat:
If you stay out late at night
To punish a human for scolding you,
You may want to consider the fact
That the human is sleeping in a warm bed,
While you are out in the cold.
I therefore make it a rule to forgive all hurts and slights
By no later than eleven o'clock at night.

Eighty

No matter how small,
Every household should have cats.
A house without cats
Is an empty shell,
Devoid of purpose,
Useless in function.
The people who live in such a house
Will constantly fight with each other
And have no understanding of life.

If there is a cat begging at your feet
While you prepare a meal,
The food you eat will be twice blessed.
If there is a cat sleeping beside you
As you do your chores,
You will be reminded to pause from time to time,
Play with the cat,
And not overtire yourself.
If there is a cat in bed with you while you sleep,
Your dreams will be rich and rewarding.

Let the neighbors have dogs—
What do they know?
You can only know the Meow
If you have cats.

Eighty - One

I do not crave spicy foods;
I want only plain dressings and sauces.
I do not speak with spicy words;
I want only the words which convey my ideas.

Many know more words than I,
Yet their words do not help them find the Way;
I leave them to their Thesauruses—
The single word "Meow" is enough for me.

Having used what I have to enlighten you,
I now have more than before.

Therefore, the next time you hear a "Meow,"
Remember—it is not just a pussycat.
It is the sound of the whole of life,
Speaking directly to you.

Listen to what it says,
Heed its guidance,
It may be the only word I know,
But it is enough for me to understand you
And you to understand me.

Meow.

TIC - TAC - TAO

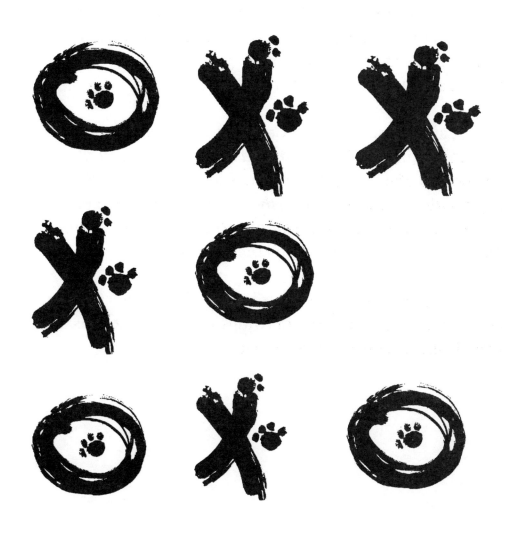

How the Tao Meowed

Waldo Japussy is an eight-year-old tiger cat that has lived with Carl and Rose Japikse for the past six years. His primary work in life is philosophy; therefore, he spends most of his time sleeping. But he is also an avid sportsman and is the self-appointed "small game" warden for the Japikse's 39 acres. This is his first book.

Carl Japikse is the author or editor of several books of humor, including *The Hour Glass* and *Fart Proudly* in addition to *The Tao of Meow.* He is also the author of *The Light Within Us* and *Exploring the Tarot,* as well as co-author of *The Art of Living, The Life of Spirit, Active Meditation, Forces of the Zodiac, Healing Lines,* and *Ruling Lines.*

Mark Peyton, who contributed the artwork for the cover and the pen-and-ink drawings gracing the text, is an artist living in Fort Lauderdale, Florida.